THE JOAN WALSH ANGLUND COLORING·BOOK

RANDOM HOUSE 🏠 NEW YORK

FOR EMILY'S SUMMER FRIENDS
Aurora, Aaron, Mary, Leigh, Will,
Ward, Cara, Christina, Jacy, Megan, Stuart,
Chip, Jamie, and Carolyn

"Wake up, Adam!" says Emily.
"The sun is rising!"

"Good morning, toys!" says Emily.

"I'm king of the castle!" says Adam.

We make Valentines for our friends...

and then we mail them.

Emily and Adam feed the hen
and her chicks every day.

Soon it will be Easter!

Adam finds a pretty Easter egg.

Emily plants a rosebush.

Who will buy these pretty flowers?

We are having a party!

We dance...

and we sing. "Happy Birthday, Emily!"

We seesaw up and down.

Adam goes fishing.

It's fun to blow bubbles—

and watch them drift away!

We float in our boat...

and play on the beach.

On a windy day our kites fly high!

Puppet shows are fun.

Emily has a picnic lunch.

Adam stays dry on a rock in the river.

"I can swim!" says Adam.

We roller-skate in the park.

Off to the Fourth of July parade!

Emily and Adam enjoy the campfire with their friends.

It's apple-picking time!

Now we have enough apples to make pies.

In the fall we go to school.

This is my book.

I can write my name.

Halloween will soon be here. We pick lots of pumpkins.

Emily is a princess.

Adam is a prince.

Trick-or-treating is fun!

Emily bakes cookies.

Gobble, gobble! The turkey likes to eat corn.

We celebrate Thanksgiving with our family.

What a handsome snowman!

Whoosh! Emily and Adam fly down the hillside!

In winter we feed the birds...

and we go ice skating.

Emily and Adam are taking a trip.

Visiting Grandma is always fun.

There's time for some last-minute shopping.

Here's Santa Claus!

We put pretty ornaments on our Christmas tree.

Adam got a hobby-horse for Christmas!

Grandmother tells us a story
before we go to sleep.

Good night, Emily!

Good night, Adam!